WOMEN EXPLORERS

Perils, Pistols, and Petticoats

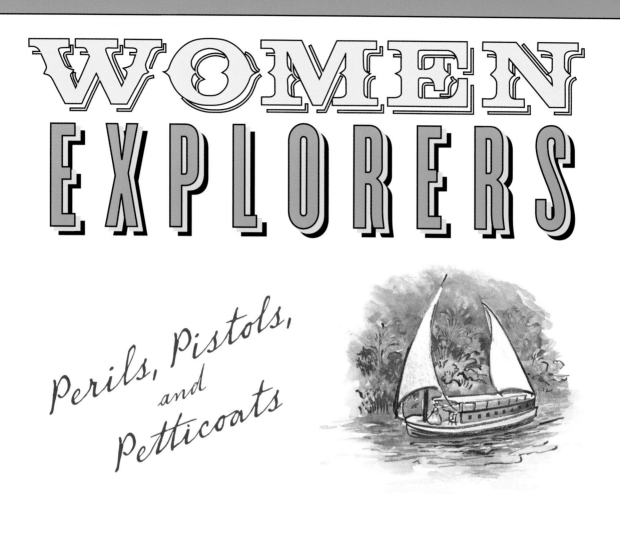

Julie Cummins

illustrated by

Cheryl Harness

PUFFIN BOOKS

To the two Stephanies in my life: Stephanie L.,
who loves to explore new ideas, and Stephanie M.,
who never shies from challenges or adventures
J.C.

To Natty of the Northern Kingdom
C.H.

PUFFIN BOOKS
An imprint of Penguin Random House LLC
375 Hudson Street
New York, New York 10014

First published in the United States of America by Dial Books for Young Readers,
a division of Penguin Young Readers Group, 2012
Published by Puffin Books, an imprint of Penguin Random House LLC, 2015

THE LIBRARY OF CONGRESS HAS CATALOGED THE DIAL BOOKS EDITION AS FOLLOWS:
Cummins, Julie.
Women explorers: perils, pistols, and petticoats / Julie Cummins ; illustrated by Cheryl Harness.
p. cm.
ISBN: 978-0-8037-3713-6 (hardcover)
I. Women explorers—Biography—Juvenile literature. I. Harness, Cheryl, ill. II. Title.
G200.C85 2012
910.92'52—dc23
2011021627

Puffin Books ISBN 978-0-14-751736-4

Manufactured in China

1 3 5 7 9 10 8 6 4 2

CONTENTS

INTRODUCTION

CLOSE YOUR EYES and name the first explorer that comes to mind. You probably said Christopher Columbus, or Henry Hudson, or even Vasco da Gama. Chances are highly unlikely that you named a woman. Yet there were many women who braved the dangers of jungles, glaciers, headhunters, cannibals, giant spiders, crocodiles, raging waterfalls, disease, extreme weather, and primitive conditions. Some journeyed alone with little more than a string hammock, while others traveled in lavish style with silver, china, and servants.

Why haven't we heard their names? The answer is: It's a sign of their times. The daring men who ventured into the great unknown are celebrated, but the many intrepid and brave women who faced the same kinds of challenges were saddled with gender barriers, societal disapproval, and second-class status: Females belonged at home!

The following ten women were born before 1900, at a time when proper ladies simply did not go gallivanting around the world to explore new territories or undiscovered places. Full-length dresses, hats, and gloves were the approved attire, not split skirts for riding camels or donkeys, or trousers for climbing mountains. Heaven forbid that a proper lady would use her parasol to fend off an attacking crocodile by ramming it down the crocodile's throat!

The daring-do of these dauntless women resulted in contributions to science, geography, history, and cultural understanding. They played an integral role in the history of exploration by organizing and financing expeditions, leading voyages themselves, and writing literary records of their adventures. They captured the wonders they saw on film, in photographs, and in diaries and books. They have been overlooked for far too long. So sally forth and meet these daring dames.

"The lure of exploration . . .
continues to be one of the strongest lodestars
of the human spirit and will be so
while there is the rim of an unknown horizon
in this world or the next."

FREYA STARK, *The Zodiac Arch 1968*

LOUISE ARNER BOYD

From Parties to Polar Bears

I T'S A LONG WAY from the wealthy, privileged life of a debutante in San Francisco to an explorer's life in the Arctic. Yet Louise Boyd journeyed back and forth between those two worlds—many times.

Her family's affluence provided Louise with governesses,

private schools, rifle shooting lessons, and horse riding. The one thing the Boyds' money couldn't buy was good health: Both of Louise's brothers died in their teens and by 1920 her father and mother had both died as well, leaving Louise all alone at age thirty-two—with three million dollars, a mansion, and control of the family investment business.

Running an investment firm was not her dream; Louise loved poring over geography books and wanted to travel. Her first trip was by chauffeured motorcar through France and Belgium, but she longed to visit less traveled parts. Louise found the love of her life on her next trip. Sailing on a Norwegian tourist boat, she glimpsed the Arctic regions for the first time, marveling that "Far north, hidden behind grim barriers of pack ice, are lands that hold one spellbound . . . the awesome immensity of lonely mountains, fiords, and glaciers."

Her fascination with the icebound world resulted in seven expeditions to the Arctic that she planned, led, and financed. The novelty of her first journey to a cluster of isolated islands in the Arctic Ocean made local headlines: *"San Francisco Woman in Arctic . . . to hunt polar bears, seals, and other Arctic animals."* And she did: Louise shot three seals and eleven polar bears, including one that charged her at forty feet.

On her second expedition, Louise changed course when she heard that her hero, Roald Amundsen, was missing. Roald was a famous Norwegian explorer who had been the first person to reach the South Pole. Now he'd disappeared while leading an aerial rescue mission to the North Pole to search for the crew of a downed Italian blimp. Louise joined the massive search of the Arctic seas that lasted three months and covered ten thousand miles.

The world held its breath as people waited for daily press bulletins.

Several of the missing Italians were eventually discovered alive, but sadly, Roald Amundsen himself was never found.

Louise decided that she would collect scientific data of this unknown region on her future voyages, and the American Geographical Society financially supported her geographic research. She spared no expense, outfitting her ship with a library, a darkroom for her photographic gear, a room for her maid, and one for the latest scientific equipment, including an echo-sounding machine that measured the depth of the sea. She was among the first to use this tool.

Louise was an expert photographer, and the detailed maps made from her pictures played a role in World War II. The U.S. government hired her as a consultant but delayed the publication of her book on hydrographic studies in 1937–38 because the military didn't want the previously uncharted information to fall into the hands of German enemies.

Transporting her camera equipment across icebergs was a slippery slope. The craggy terrain was hazardous, and the wildlife was equally dangerous. When she was photographing, Louise had to be on constant guard for attacks by rogue musk ox. In herds they avoided people, but a lone bull could charge at full speed. Luckily, their rank odor wasn't the only thing the musk oxen left behind. They also rubbed their wool off on the bushes and boulders, and Louise collected this bounty to make sweaters and mufflers.

Louise led two lives: sophisticated, stylishly dressed socialite who always wore a hat and a fresh flower in her lapel, and pioneer explorer who wore boots and breeches to bed aboard ship but always powdered her nose before going up on deck. Thanks to Louise Boyd, the Arctic was no longer only a man's world.

NELLIE CASHMAN

Go West, Young Lady

PICTURE A GOLD PROSPECTOR playing a role in the exploration of the Canadian wilderness. You're probably imagining a grizzled man with a beard, right? Surprise! Nellie Cashman was a persistent, compassionate woman who shared her "wealth"—in her inimitable way.

Nellie was born in Ireland during the potato famine of the mid-1800s. To escape starvation, her family immigrated to the United States. Nellie swore that she would never be poor again. She dreamed of making lots of money and helping people. And she did both.

Her family moved to Boston, where Nellie worked as a bellhop in a hotel—a job usually held by men, but available to her, since many had enlisted in the Civil War. Union Army General Ulysses S. Grant himself stayed there at times. He told Nellie "the West needs people like you" and that it was easier to make money out there. She took his advice. In 1869 Nellie and her sister went to San Francisco. After Fanny got married, Nellie went off to search for gold in Nevada, where she worked as a cook while learning to prospect.

In 1877 when gold was discovered in Cassiar, a wilderness region of British Columbia, Canada, Nellie joined the human stampede up north and became the first white woman to explore the remote area. Six other miners went with her; they all found gold, staked a claim, and left for home. On the way back, they heard that men in a mining camp were starving and suffering from scurvy, a disease caused by lack of vitamin C. Nellie immediately changed their direction to go help. Traveling by snowshoe with several pack animals carrying 1,500 pounds of food supplies, it took the miners seventy-seven days to reach the camp. Now that's lending a hand—and hoofs!

After Nellie nursed almost one hundred men back to health with nutritious food, no others died. The grateful miners rightfully called her

"Angel of the Cassiar." She was only five feet tall and weighed less than one hundred pounds, but as one miner said, "What [Nellie] lacked in height and weight, she made up for with courage and an iron will."

Her next move was to Tombstone, Arizona, which had become a silver-mining Boomtown in 1880. Nellie opened a restaurant and was known for serving cheap (but good) food to miners and free food to those without cash. Nellie Cashman's Restaurant is still in business today, located at the corner of Fifth and Toughnut Streets—a fitting location.

When gold was discovered in the Klondike territory of Canada in 1897, it called Nellie's name. She searched for gold by dog sled and on snowshoes, and her forays paid off—big! She struck it rich, distributing some of her newfound wealth to the poor and using the rest to continue her exploration as she followed the gold rush to Alaska (long before it became a state). She lived sixty miles south of the Arctic Circle, the frozen area around the North Pole. Her endurance was amazing: She survived blizzards without food or blankets and relied on homemade rafts to traverse raging rivers.

At age seventy Nellie mushed a dog team for seventeen days over 750 miles of ice and snow. This was her last incredible journey; five years later she died of pneumonia. "Tougher than two-penny nails," she was one of the first female entrepreneurs of the Old West. She was a real "gold digger" in the best sense, one who shared her riches by donating money to many charities, churches, and especially to the poor, which she had vowed never to be again.

YNES MEXIA

Going Green

YNES MEXIA'S (Eye-NEZ MEX-ee-uh) PURSUIT to discover new
plant life was as exotic as her name. For thirteen years,
she explored the wilderness of Mexico and the United States to
collect rare and unidentified plants—almost always traveling alone.
Her preference for solitude grew out of two unhappy

marriages, family turmoil, and resentment at having to care for her ailing father. He was a demanding, retired Mexican diplomat to the United States, where Ynes was born and raised. Her preference for working alone would suit her well as a field botanist.

The bug for collecting plants didn't bite her until age fifty-five, when a physical and mental breakdown made her see a doctor in San Francisco, California. Thanks to him, she regained interest in life. As therapy, she hiked and took long walks in the woods, where she developed an interest in the beautiful foliage, undergrowth, and vegetation.

Botany—the study of plants—was a new science in the early 1900s, and women were considered unsuitable for the job. Ynes had to work doubly hard to prove herself to be a valid field collector. She kept meticulous records, photographing each plant, drying it, and carefully typing notes. To ensure she had sufficient supplies, she brought roughly seventy-five pounds of paper that mules had to carry in addition to her camera and typewriter, all hauled around in far from ideal conditions.

Ynes was contemptuous of field collectors who stayed in hotels, believing it was necessary to be as far afield as possible. She preferred to set up a cot under a banana tree in a pine forest!

The Mexican government asked her to acquire plants for several herbariums, and in seven months she collected thousands of plants, mosses, ferns, herbs, shrubs, and trees, fifty of which were new species.

Not all of her exploration took place in dank, overgrown places. Ynes went from one extreme to another—from stiflingly hot Mexico to frosty Alaska. She spent part of 1928 surveying

plants in Mount McKinley National Park, all alone in a tiny cabin.

Her next pursuit was her greatest adventure: a dream journey of traveling up the Amazon River in South America. She voyaged by river steamer, riverboat, and a dugout canoe that was manned by four paddlers. For twelve days she sat on a box in the canoe, sheltered by an umbrella when it rained and wearing a sun helmet when the sun shone—until she convinced the men to build a palm-leaf cover over her box.

Life along the Amazon was filled with dangers and risks, particularly for a woman. Yet Ynes wasn't daunted by having to eat roots, roasted monkey, or parrots. She didn't even blink an eye at living with headhunters! For three months, she lived with the Aguarunas (ah-gwah-ROO-nahs), an Amazon Indian tribe who believed that enemies caused sickness and death, so they killed them, cut off their heads, and dried and shrunk them.

What must these deadly Indians have thought of this white woman living among them? Evidently she was not considered a threat due to her respectful manner. They traded fishhooks and needles, and they helped her locate plants. Strange partners!

Ynes spent two and a half years in South America and collected 65,000 plants, many of which were named after her. While others said that she had the soul of an explorer, Ynes called herself the "Wilful [sic] Wanderer." In her humble words, she was ". . . a nature lover and a bit of an adventuress [who] passed unharmed through [regions] reported to be infected with bandits, tarantulas, and wild animals."

However you describe her, one thing is certain: She gave meaning to the term "going green" long before its time.

LUCY EVELYN CHEESMAN

A Bug up Her Sleeve

SPIDERS, SNAKES, AND SNAILS, OH MY! Many mothers would throw up their hands in dismay if their daughters brought home such creepy crawlies, but Lucy Evelyn Cheesman's childhood in an upper-class Edwardian home was far from typical. Her mother actually encouraged Lucy and her siblings to bring home all kinds of insects, wild things, and bugs to study, like the glowworms Evelyn collected to figure out what made them glow.

Evelyn desperately wanted to become a veterinarian when she grew up, but she was told that as a woman, she would not be admitted to vet school. So she was delighted when she was offered a job as the keeper of the insect house at the Zoological Society in London. Their menagerie of bugs fascinated her, and she discovered that she had a flair for sharing her enthusiasm with others.

In 1923, at the age of forty-two, she received an offer to join a zoological expedition to the South Pacific. Evelyn jumped at the chance to fulfill a dream. But when the group arrived in Tahiti, she set off on her own with only insect trays, a string hammock, and some basic necessities. Foolhardy? Maybe, but to the amazement of her family and friends back home, "frail" Evelyn made eight more solo expeditions to the South Seas over the next thirty years and proved to be tough enough to survive bouts of malaria and dengue fever, as well as deadly snakes, crocodiles, and giant spiders.

On one trek she started to cross a clearing draped with webs of the huge, majestic-looking Nephila spiders. Thinking she could brush through the webs, she pushed ahead, only to become totally entangled:
"I even tried to bite the threads, but that was useless. All around hung spiders of all ages, some near my face. I did not think them handsome anymore." Finally, she cut through the webs, strand by strand, with a nail file from her pocket. It took her several hours and all the while the spiders sat waiting for their dinner—her! Sound like a scene from an Indiana Jones movie? After that frightening and very real encounter, Evelyn was never without a machete.

As shocking as it was for a middle-aged white woman to go exploring in primitive areas under primitive conditions, even more incredible was the fact that Evelyn often lived with cannibals! Why wasn't she in danger? Their friendly relationship was due to the fact that "they were in the superior position of offering me instruction. Thus, a very special link was forged between us when they found that I did not attempt to press alien ideas on them."

However, their barbaric eating habits were alien to Evelyn, who preferred coconuts to human meat. Following one tribal skirmish after which the natives ate the dead, Evelyn asked one of her helpers if he would have eaten her if she had been killed. Of course, he replied; eating someone had nothing to do with friendship, but with preventing the person's ghost from haunting them. The cannibals believed Evelyn had a strong spirit and that eating her when she died would keep her ghost away. Gulp!

At only five foot two, wearing a bush suit with shoes and stockings, this petite woman went into places where no white woman had ever been seen. She wrote about her fascinating adventures and stories of insect life in a dozen books, including some for children. Evelyn once said, "Discomfort and danger are part of being a scientist." Neither one dampened Evelyn's enthusiasm for a life with bugs.

ANNIE SMITH PECK

How High Can You Climb?

WOMEN MOUNTAIN CLIMBERS? Shocking! Scandalous! Certainly *not* an activity for ladies in the late 1800s or early 1900s, no way! Yet one American woman chose to challenge both the prudish dictates of society and mountainous heights in faraway places.

Annie Smith Peck was born in New England, the daughter of wealthy and influential parents. They were descendants of Roger Williams, the founder of their home state of Rhode Island. She was well schooled with a strong, proper upbringing that led her to set her goals high—really high.

In 1885, Annie was the first woman admitted to teach at the American School of Classical Studies in Athens, Greece. On her way there she glimpsed the "majestic, awe-inspiring peak" of the Matterhorn Mountain in the Alps, and she vowed to return one day and climb it. Ten years later, she did just that, becoming the third woman to scale Matterhorn in the nineteenth century. Having reached that goal, her greatest ambition became "to conquer a virgin peak, to attain some height where no man had previously stood."

Her climbing outfit was a hip-length woolen tunic, knickerbockers (knee breeches), puttees (leg wrappings), and a saucer-shaped felt hat tied with a veil. Her pants outfit made her a celebrity and the Singer Sewing Machine Company included a photo of her with climbing irons and rope with every new machine they sold.

Several failed attempts to scale mountains in South America kept her goal out of reach. First, she had to find funding for her expeditions. Her appeals to newspapers, magazines, and friends brought mixed responses; skeptics and doubters advised her to stay home, to which she replied, "My home is where my trunk is."

Money wasn't the only obstacle. Annie also had to deal with cold feet! Not her own, but those of the male guides she hired for protection and scientific documentation. Either they couldn't handle the severe weather

and physical demands, or they quit because they resented taking orders from a woman.

On August 31, 1908, in bone-chilling cold, Annie stood squinting up at the great Andean mountain, Mount Huascaran in Peru. After five failed attempts, she was determined to conquer the massive, snow-covered heights towering thousands of feet high. To protect her face from the extreme cold, she wore a woolen face mask—and painted a mustache on it! Most likely the men in her group failed to find it funny.

The ascent was dreadfully dangerous, but the descent was "a horrible nightmare." When Annie planted her feet back on firm ground, she shook her fist at the mountain. She had finally beaten it and she vowed never to return.

However, not everyone reveled in her achievement. When another female climber, Fanny Bullock Workman, heard of Annie's claim that she had reached a record height between 23,000 and 24,000 feet, she was enraged. Feisty and competitive, Fanny immediately challenged the claim by hiring scientists to go to Peru to calculate the height. Who won? The official height was set at 22,205 feet. Nevertheless, Annie's achievements were recognized when a mountain was named for her.

Annie was a suffragette who saw herself as setting an example. On a trek she made in 1911, she planted a pennant that said: "Votes for women." (It would take nine years before women were allowed to vote.) Her passion for climbing mountains left a legacy not only for women explorers but women worldwide.

ALEXANDRINE TINNÉ

Mystery of the Nile

IF YOUR FATHER DIED when you were ten and left you the richest heiress in your country, how would you spend your money? Most girls born to wealthy Dutch parents would have chosen high society life, but Alexandrine Tinné decided to travel to unknown places.

She and her mother had traveled widely in Europe, but Alexandrine wanted to explore uncharted territory. Inspired by the male explorers of Africa, especially Dr. David Livingston, she was only nineteen when she embarked on the greatest quest of her time: searching for the source of the Nile River.

Expressing a typical reaction to this improper behavior by a Victorian lady, Samuel Baker, another African explorer, said: "There are Dutch ladies traveling without any gentlemen. . . they must be demented. . . they really must be mad. All the natives are naked as the day they were born! Shocking indeed."

Alexandrine spent the next fifteen years becoming a skilled photographer, botanical illustrator, and naturalist, venturing into places where no woman had set foot before and becoming one of the first—and certainly the most colorful—explorers of the Nile.

For her first trip, Alexandrine hired one large boat that towed two boats behind it full of provisions, but she didn't make it very far. A large waterfall forced the group to turn back. The second trip wasn't much better. Her goal of reaching the Sudan was stopped short by the Nile cataracts, the infamous roiling rapids above the Aswan Dam. She realized they needed more equipment and better boats.

The third time was no charm either, though it started very well. Alexandrine's mother and aunt accompanied her on her Nile expeditions and to say the women traveled in a lavish style would be an understatement. Alexandrine engaged a fleet of boats and embarked with china, silver, furniture, livestock, servants, five pet dogs (that had to be put ashore twice a day), and on Tinné's personal riverboat, her grand piano!

In twelve weeks' time, they reached Khartoum, Sudan, but the

hazardous journey took its toll: bad weather, illness, and fierce mosquitoes that bit their faces, which swelled beyond recognition. All three women came down with Nile swamp fever, and only Alexandrine survived.

In spite of her grief and guilt over being responsible for her mother's and aunt's deaths, Alexandrine persevered and pushed on with six boats. However, tropical storms and more illness finally forced her to give up her search for the source of the Nile.

Alexandrine's passion for exploring, however, wasn't deterred. She turned her attention to North Africa and planned to be the first woman to cross the Sahara Desert. Her first attempt was unsuccessful, and her second try would be fatal: Despite having a letter of safe conduct from a Tuareg chieftain, Alexandrine was murdered.

Stories vary: Some sources say her camel drivers murdered her en route for valuables that they thought she had or that her guides believed her iron water tanks were filled with gold; others claim she was caught in a bloody political conflict between local Tuareg chiefs. But the most troubling account is that she was attacked by tribesmen and when she raised her hand in peace, they cut it off and she bled to death. We'll never know which version is the truth, because Alexandrine's body was never found.

She would be proud of this tribute from the man who had inspired her. Dr. Livingston said: "But none rises higher in my estimation than the Dutch lady, Miss Tinné, who after the severest afflictions, nobly persevered in the teeth of every difficulty."

Even though her life and exploration career were cut short, Alexandrine's efforts rivaled those of leading male explorers of her day.

DELIA JULIA DENNING AKELEY

Africa, from Dawn to Tusk

WHEN DELIA DENNING ran away from her parents' farm in Wisconsin at age thirteen, she wasn't dreaming of becoming a big-game hunter. But it was that first taste of independence that led her to Milwaukee and the man who would transform her life into one of exploration.

Carl Akeley was a sculptor at the Milwaukee Art Museum when the Field Museum of Natural History in Chicago hired him as a taxidermist to prepare realistic exhibits. Delia immersed herself in Carl's work as he perfected the art of preserving animal carcasses to look lifelike, first becoming his assistant and then his wife.

In 1905 the museum commissioned the couple to go to East Africa to collect elephants for an exhibit. Tracking elephants was far from easy—the huge animals could cover fifty miles a day through swamps and rugged terrain. To keep up, Delia often walked all day, climbing steep ridges, sliding down slippery slopes, or pushing through tangled overgrowth. She outfitted herself in safari togs: boots and pith helmet, but underneath? "I always wore silk underwear in the jungle."

On the expeditions, Delia not only had to manage the camp, care for her often-ailing husband, and hunt for food, but she also had to shoot and preserve the specimens for the museum. Though she had no previous experience with guns, Delia turned out to be a crackerjack marksman. In her words, "scarcely breathing, and with legs trembling so I could hardly stand, I waited for the elephant to move forward. Dimly through the mist the dark shape came slowly . . . exposing a splendid pair of tusks and a great flapping ear which was my target. With nerves keyed to the point of action I fired, and the first elephant I shot at fell lifeless."

The splendid beast weighed several tons, stood ten feet ten inches tall, and carried 180 pounds of ivory. It took twelve hours to remove and preserve the skin, which weighed a ton and a quarter by itself. Delia's prize mammoth bull elephant was shipped intact to the Field Museum in 1906 and is still on display today.

Delia and Carl were divorced in 1923, but Delia struck out on her own and continued to make a name for herself. Sponsored by the Brooklyn Museum to ship back mammal specimens and native crafts from Africa, she was the first endorsed woman to lead a safari alone.

Delia allowed herself just a few luxuries in the jungle. She used a collapsible rubber tub for her evening bath, and she also made her own bread, using native banana beer in place of yeast and baking it in a pan over an open fire.

At the age of fifty, she became the first woman explorer to cross Africa from coast to coast. It took eleven months to journey from the Indian Ocean to the Belgian Congo (now Zaire) on this hazardous trip, traveling first by dugout canoe and then by camel. Delia took hundreds of photographs and made her own negatives to document the experience. But her biggest and most adventurous challenge was yet to come: a search for the elusive Pygmies. And against all odds, she found them.

The Bambutes (bam-BOO-tees) were a Pygmy tribe with the average adult standing only four feet high. Upon meeting them, she presented them with salt, tobacco, and a red balloon. Because of her white hair and skin, they thought she had magic power and welcomed her into their community. In the three months that Delia lived and hunted with the Pygmies, she took 1,500 photographs and 5,000 feet of film. She also spent time with the children, teaching them to jump rope with forest vines. But she had to draw the line somewhere: When the natives wanted her to hunt naked because her clothes made too much noise, she politely refused.

A woman with an indomitable spirit, Delia died at age ninety-five having loved her adopted land of wild beasts, wild terrain, and wild people.

VIOLET CRESSY-MARCKS

"Shrinking Violet?"— Not This Lady!

To say that Violet Cressy-Marcks traveled far and wide is an understatement! This amateur psychologist made eight trips around the world—alone for all but one. Her pursuits helped crack the taboos of women traveling solo.

What compelled Violet to explore is anyone's guess. When people asked her how she could be brave enough to risk her life making trips that carried threats of serious illness, food shortages, and dangers from natives, primitive conditions, and political unrest, she assured them that there was a greater risk living in Europe, which exposed one to thieves, lunatics, and accidents!

In 1928 and 1929 she traveled by reindeer-drawn sled across Norway and Finland to northwest Russia, above the Arctic Circle. Next, she traveled to South America by sailing a boat up the Amazon River, riding a mule over the Andes Mountains, and taking a train to Lima, Peru. Violet arrived with multiple trunks and suitcases—way too many! She sent a number of items back to England, discarded others along the way, and gave away dresses to the Peruvian women. Even so, it took eight mules to carry her scientific instruments, guns, cameras, canvas bath, medicine chest, and tent.

Too much baggage was the least of Violet's problems in the Andes. A snakebite on her leg became infected, forcing her to walk painfully through rain and mud. At one hut, a man gave her food and a poncho to wear while she washed out her dirty, soggy clothes and hung them to dry on bushes. During the night the wind blew them into the fire—only her shoes survived! Fortunately, she had a silk frock bunched up in her hammock. When she finally reached Lima (looking quite bedraggled), she checked into a fancy hotel. For the rest of the trip, she hired a bus.

The only time Violet didn't travel by herself was on her sixth

trip, to China, when she took along her second husband. She studied the political situation while Francis collected information on Chinese agriculture (though he would only eat European food). She thought he was an excellent traveling companion except that he "refused to kill his own lice."

During their long stay in China, Violet hoped to interview Mao Tse-tung, the Communist leader of the People's Republic of China. She was on her way to the war front when her train was bombed. All the passengers, including Violet, fled to the fields while the train shunted back and forth to avoid the bombs. Amazingly, there were few casualties. Violet eventually arrived safe but shaken and got her interview with Mao at Red Army headquarters; it lasted five hours.

No stranger to the front lines, she went on to serve as a driver and news correspondent for a London newspaper during World War II, covering events in China. Her perseverance took her to Germany, where she reported on the famous Nuremberg war crime trials.

Violet made her eighth and last round-the-world journey in 1956. Following a whirlwind of worldwide travel, she died in 1970. Her obituary in the *London Times* said: "No contemporary British woman equaled or indeed approached her record of adventurous journeys in unfamiliar lands." This lady was definitely no "shrinking violet."

FREYA STARK

Arabian Nights and Days

FREYA STARK'S TRAVELS began as a baby when her mother carried her across the Dolomite Mountains in Italy in a basket. Her upbringing was unconventional for the time, as her parents mostly lived separate lives. Both were painters, but her Italian mother and English father each chose to live in his or her homeland.

When she was twelve, Freya suffered a hair-raising accident, literally. Her mother owned a carpet factory and one day Freya's long hair got caught in the machinery. She was yanked off her feet and half of her scalp was torn away. It took four months for her to recover and even though skin was grafted onto her face, she was still left with ugly scars. To make them less noticeable, she draped her hair to cover the scarred side of her face and also wore long scarves and large hats that became her trademark look.

When World War I broke out in 1914, she immediately left the University of London to train as a nurse. During her training, she caught typhoid fever and almost died. It was the first of many illnesses that would plague her throughout her life. When she recovered, she wanted to travel, to go places with lots of "space, distance, history, and danger." Muslim countries intrigued her, so she decided to learn Arabic. She made her first visit to Syria in 1927 when she was thirty-four, followed by Lebanon the next year. This trip became a compass point in her life, when she fell in love with desert travel.

"I never imagined that my first sight of the desert would come as such a shock of beauty and enslave me right away." With her appetite whetted for more travel in the Middle East, she moved to Baghdad in 1929 and rented a room with an Iraqi shoemaker to practice Arabic with his family.

The legends she'd heard about assassins in one remote, mountainous part of Persia fascinated Freya. They were a medieval Islamic cult of warrior mystics, who allegedly lived in castles among distant rugged peaks. She found several ruins of their mountaintop castles, but her excitement was

overcome by gravely serious cases of dysentery and malaria. Freya survived, but had other close calls: a heart attack while visiting the walled cities in Turkey and a case of measles while exploring the early centers of spice and incense trade. Both times she had to be rescued by the Royal Air Force.

In 1936, and in better health, Freya headed to the southern coast of the Arabian Peninsula, a crossroad of people, cultures, and religions of history past. She remarked, "A journey without history is like a portrait of an old face without its wrinkles."

During World War II, Freya's expertise and information from her forays greatly benefited the British War Office, improving their maps of the areas and supplying details for British Intelligence.

After years of travel, Freya realized she could make a living by writing about her journeys. Her first book, *Baghdad Sketches*, was published in 1933 and *The Valley of the Assassins* the next year. All together she published a total of twenty books.

By 1972, Freya's fame had reached such heights that Queen Elizabeth II of England made her a Dame of the British Empire, the equivalent of being knighted.

Proving her belief that "curiosity ought to increase as one gets older," she was in her seventies when she went to China for the first time; at seventy-six she toured Afghanistan; and at age eighty-nine she was filmed by the BBC television network as she rode a donkey to the base of Annapurna Mountain in Nepal!

Despite all of her health problems, Freya survived to be a century old. She lived up to her own quote: As a "grand dame" she had the soul of an explorer whose journeys left a mark on history.

DAISY BATES

Walk on the Wild Side

THE SONG TITLE "WALK ON THE WILD SIDE" describes the unusual life of Daisy Bates, an extraordinary and eccentric woman who married three times, had a son, lived in primitive conditions in the Australian outback, and became one of the best-known ethnologists (a person who studies human culture) in history. In fact, everything about Daisy was controversial, and her behavior was considered quite improper in the prim Victorian times.

At the age of twenty-one she emigrated from Ireland to Australia. Daisy was clever enough not to let hints of a scandal or her orphan youth deter her from high ambitions as she conveniently reinvented her personal history from humble governess to heiress-traveler to woman of science, a trait that became a pattern throughout her dual life.

Records show that she married a poet and horseman in 1884, but after a short time she threw him out because he failed to pay for the wedding and stole livestock.

Soon after her first marriage failed, Daisy moved to New South Wales and became engaged, but the man died before they could marry. In 1885 she lost her heart to a handsome cattle drover, but that marriage too was a mistake. He was no match for her energetic nature, and she found his lifestyle boring. Fed up, she placed her eight-year-old son in boarding school and left for England, where she arrived penniless. Always resourceful, though, she found a job as a journalist.

At about the same time, a letter was published in *The Times* (a London newspaper) that criticized the cruelty of West Australian settlers to Aborigines. Daisy wrote to *The Times*, offering to make full investigations and report the results to them. Her offer was accepted and she sailed back to Australia in 1899. It was there that her other wild side came out.

Daisy was so fascinated with the Australian Aborigines that she spent thirty-five years of her life studying their history, culture, rites, beliefs, and customs. She tirelessly fought for Aboriginal welfare, setting up camps to feed, clothe, and nurse the transient population, often using her own money, even selling her cattle station to cover the costs. Another

expense was her own health, which suffered from a diet without fresh vegetables.

Wherever she traveled around the country in the outback, Daisy just pitched her tent and set up her typewriter. Ignoring the primitive conditions, Daisy persisted in dressing in proper Victorian fashion that included long skirts, boots, gloves, and a hat with a veil. Over cups of tea, she built a relationship of trust with the Aborigines, and the natives called her *Kabbarli*, meaning "grandmother." Despite the proper dress, one of the legendary stories about her claimed that she always wore pistols and threatened policemen if she caught them mistreating "her" Aborigines. She was some awesome Aussie, pistol-packin' mama!

The "Great White Queen of the Never Never," as the press called Daisy, wrote more than 270 articles about Aboriginal life for newspapers and journals. Her accounts were among the first serious studies of Aboriginal culture. In 1904 the Australian government appointed her to research Aboriginal customs, languages, and dialects, a task that took her six years. Her last publication, *The Passing of the Aborigines*, became a European best seller despite controversy over its later-disproved claims that Aborigines practiced cannibalism.

In recognition of her work, Daisy was named Honorary Protector of Aborigines, and royalty visited three times to see firsthand her welfare at work. She was so famous that she even had an opera written about her.

After she died at age ninety-one, facts came to light that proved Daisy had reinvented her own history. Unlucky in love, was she a heroine, a charming eccentric, a storyteller, or a passionate woman dedicated to a cause? Sources don't agree, but one thing is certain: Daisy walked the wild side among the Aboriginal people and became their godmother, their guardian, and advocate.

WHY IS IT THAT WOMEN EXPLORERS ARE MOSTLY UNKNOWN? Their endeavors were just as dangerous and daring as those of male explorers, yet history books have slighted them. The ten women chosen for this book made significant contributions to the world with their quests of exploration. Born before 1900, not only did they brave society's disapproval of women crossing the line into male territory, but they also had to brace themselves for the physical demands of climbing new heights. This was an era when even the idea of women wearing pants was scandalous, yet these "adventurettes" were genuine adventurers, equal to any male bravado.

The challenges in writing this companion book to *Women Daredevils: Thrills, Chills, and Frills*, were different from those I came upon while researching female daredevils, as hardly any books focused on them as a subject. On the other hand, there are sporadic books devoted to women explorers that include a bevy of women who climbed mountains and conquered the unknown, which made it hard to select just ten explorers. It was a case of so many impressive women, but so little page space. In choosing, I tried to cover a broad expanse of territories and vary the type of exploration, but the one thing these women had in common was their determination and fortitude as they traversed the world from one end to the other.

MORE WOMEN WHO LEFT FOOTPRINTS ON THE ROADS OF EXPLORATION

ALL OF THESE WOMEN proved that female explorers could be just as daring and adventurous as men!

HARRIET CHALMERS ADAMS
American, 1875–1937
One of the best-known explorers of South America, Harriet became a war correspondent for *Harper's Magazine* in 1916 and was the only woman allowed to visit the trenches in France. In 1927 she fell from a sea wall in the Balearic Islands in eastern Spain, broke her back, and spent two years strapped to a board. Despite being told she would never walk again, she recovered and continued to explore in Spain and Asia Minor.

ANNIE MONTAGUE ALEXANDER
American, 1867–1950
Known as the patroness of paleontology, the study of fossils, Anne funded numer-

ous expeditions, collected prehistoric camel skeletons, and explored mountains. She celebrated her eightieth birthday while on a plant-hunting trip in the remote mountains of Baja, California.

LUCY ATKINSON
English, 1826–1863
An adventurer by nature, Lucy was a British governess in Russia when she married an English artist. They traveled to remote regions of Asiatic Russia, where they were guests of nomadic tribesmen. While there, she astonished the tribesmen with her masterful horse racing and tenacity at bathing in icy mountain streams three times a day. After she gave birth to a baby boy while in the mountains, she even dipped him into the frigid water.

FLORENCE VON SASS BAKER
Balkan, 1841–1916
Florence's life of exploring uncharted territories in Africa with her husband was filled with mystery and romance. They solved many age-old mysteries of the Nile River, tried to abolish slave trade, and gathered plant samples for scientific research.

AGNES DEAN CAMERON
Canadian, 1863–1912
Agnes's adventurous spirit spurred her to leave her position as the first female high school teacher in British Columbia, Canada, in order to explore the Canadian wilderness. She survived mosquitoes, moose, and rapids, and was never without her photo equipment and typewriter.

ALEXANDRA DAVID-NEÉL
French, 1868–1969
A born rebel and wanderer, Alexandra deliberately ignored society's expectations of women to explore unmapped, remote areas of China and Tibet, where no Western woman had gone. She often traveled disguised as a beggar woman. Alexandra shocked everyone when she moved into a cave in Sikkim, near the Tibetan border, for more than a year during the period of 1914–1916, in order to further her spirituality.

MARGUERITE BAKER HARRISON
American, 1879–1967
Housewife, reporter, spy, and film producer—these were only some of the lives that Marguerite led. Combining exploration with moviemaking, she made an epic film of the nomadic Bakhtiari people of Persia (now Iran) after traveling with them on their annual migration in the 1920s. She was a reporter who became a spy and was imprisoned twice in the Soviet Union, the longer imprisonment lasting ten months.

MARY KINGSLEY
American, 1862–1900
One of the few widely known women explorers, Mary left England at age thirty for West Africa. While there, she collected zoological specimens of fish and researched tribal "fetishes" (small objects believed to have magical power). She became an authority on native culture by traveling as a trader among the black people of coastal forests. Undaunted by primitive condi-

tions, she ate snake and crocodile, traveled by canoe, and used her parasol to fend off a hippo. She died at the early age of thirty-eight of typhoid fever.

BLAIR NILES
American, 1880–1959

Married twice, Blair became a traveler and explorer through her husbands' work. Her first husband was the curator of ornithology at the New York Zoological Society, and for ten years he and Blair made bird-hunting expeditions into remote areas of Mexico, South America, and the Far East. Her second husband was an architect and photographer, and they traveled together to the island penal colonies in French Guiana. Blair was the first white woman to visit Devil's Island, and the story she and her husband published about the experience made them famous.

MARIANNE NORTH
English, 1830–1890

A botanical illustrator, Marianne searched for plants all over the world and then painted them. In Brazil she took weeklong treks on a mule amid snakes and spiders as big as sparrows. No matter how dangerous or harsh the conditions were, Marianne painted every day.

SELECTED BIBLIOGRAPHY

McLOONE, MARGO. *Women Explorers in Asia*. Capstone, 1997.
Women Explorers in Africa. Capstone, 1997.
Women Explorers in North and South America. Capstone, 1997.
Women Explorers in Polar Regions. Capstone, 1997.
OLDS, ELIZABETH FAGG. *Women of the Four Winds*. Houghton Mifflin, 1985.
POLK, MILBRY AND MARY TIEGREEN. *Women of Discovery*. Clarkson/Potter, 2001.
STEFOFF, REBECCA. *Women of the World: Women Travelers and Explorers*. Oxford University Press, 1992.
TINGLING, MARION. *Women into the Unknown*. Greenwood Press, 1989.

WEBSITES

www.distinguishedwomen.com/subject/explore.html
http://ca.encarta.msn.com/list_yougogirl/You_Go_Girl_7_Women_Explorers.html
http://womenshistory.about.com/od/gifts/tp/aatpexplorers.htm